Data Analytics

Applicable Data Analysis to Advance Any Business Using the Power of Data Driven Analytics

Jeff Reed

© **Copyright 2017 by Jeff Reed. All rights reserved.**

This document is geared towards providing exact and reliable information in regards to the topic and issue covered. The publication is sold with the idea that the publisher is not required to render accounting, officially permitted, or otherwise, qualified services. If advice is necessary, legal or professional, a practiced individual in the profession should be ordered.

- From a Declaration of Principles which was accepted and approved equally by a Committee of the American Bar Association and a Committee of Publishers and Associations.

In no way is it legal to reproduce, duplicate, or transmit any part of this document in either electronic means or in printed format. Recording of this publication is strictly prohibited and any storage of this document is not allowed unless with written permission from the publisher. All rights reserved.

The information provided herein is stated to be truthful and consistent, in that any liability, in terms of inattention or otherwise, by any usage or abuse of any policies, processes, or directions contained within is the solitary and utter responsibility of the recipient reader. Under no circumstances will any legal responsibility or blame be held against the publisher for any reparation, damages, or monetary loss due to the information herein, either directly or indirectly.

Respective authors own all copyrights not held by the publisher.

The information herein is offered for informational purposes solely, and is universal as so. The presentation of the information is without contract or any type of guarantee assurance.

The trademarks that are used are without any consent, and the publication of the trademark is without permission or backing by the trademark owner. All trademarks and brands within this book are for clarifying purposes only and are the owned by the owners themselves, not affiliated with this document.

Table of Contents

Introduction	1
Chapter 1 What Is Big Data And Why It Is A Big Deal	3
Chapter 2 Big Data: A Critical Key In Business Growth	18
Chapter 3 Data Analytics In The Business World	30
Chapter 4 Tools, Technologies, And Trends In Business Data Analytics	51
Chapter 5 The Importance Of Data Mining In Advancing Business	66
Chapter 6 Data Integration And Its Role In Advancing Business	77
Chapter 7 Data Visualization	94
Chapter 8 Develop Your Own Data Analytics Strategy And Action Plan	109
Conclusion	119
Other Books By Author	120

Introduction

I'm sure that you are quite familiar with the adage that knowledge is power, and this couldn't be more true in this day and age. The world today lives and breathes knowledge. The Information Age has driven the best innovations and changes in the world.

But before knowledge becomes knowledge, it comes in the form of data -- a series of nonsensical numbers and text and even abstract thought. However, once processed and analyzed, it can be converted into a powerful resource for businesses.

During World War II, the opposing forces surely invested on armaments, but they also poured resources on capturing data from enemy sources and how to make sense of them. It was processed data that decoded most of the secret messages, and it was processed data that led to the invention of the atomic bomb, which was used by the Allied Forces to end the war.

Even though we are not at war today, businesses can use processed data to compete with each other. Valuable data can be used as a competitive edge in the business to crush the competition or to advance the business.

Businesses can effectively gather data, make sense of them, and respond accordingly through big data and data analytics. I have written this book to help business owners, corporate executives, and organizational leaders to understand what data analytics is all about, the different forms of analytics you can use, and the advantages of using analytics for advancing business.

Chapter 1
What Is Big Data and Why It Is a Big Deal

Big Data refers to non-conventional strategies and innovative technologies used by businesses and organizations to capture, manage, process, and make sense of a large volume of information. While the challenge of working with data, which surpasses the computing power or storage of one computer is considered old technology, the velocity, volume, and value of this kind of computing has remarkably expanded in the previous years.

In this Chapter, we will discuss the basic concept of big data and establish common ideas, which you may come across while looking into data analytics in depth for your business. Also, we will take a generic look at some of the technologies and processes that are presently being used in this area.

Just What Is Big Data?

It is difficult to nail down an exact definition of big data as business professionals may have a different view from a data scientist. Because this book is geared towards business advantage, we can define big data as a large dataset relevant for the business. It also refers to the category of computing technologies and strategies, which are used to manage these datasets.

A large dataset refers to the volume of information that is too large to process or preserve on a single computer or conventional file systems. And because datasets may vary from one organization to another, the common scale of large datasets may continue to shift.

The basic requirements for working with big data are similar to the requirements for working with any size of dataset. But the sheer volume, the speed of processing, and the features of the data should be dealt with every phase of the process pose critical new challenges in designing business solutions. In business, data systems can be used to gain new insights and connections from massive volumes of raw data, which may not be possible using traditional tools and strategies.

Three Characteristics of Big Data

There are three characteristics of Big Data, which makes it different from the usual data processing: velocity, volume, and variety.

Velocity

The speed at which data moves through the system is the first characteristic that makes big data different from the usual data processing. Information regularly flows into the system from several sources and is usually expected to be processed in real time to obtain business insights and guide the business in making important decisions.

The focus on immediate mechanism has equipped many businesses to look away from a wave-focused strategy and move to instant streaming mechanism. In using Big Data, a business should continuously add, manage, process, and analyze information so the organization can keep up with the flow of new data and to discover valuable information right on the onset when the data is highly relevant for the business.

Volume

The immensity of the data processed could help in defining big data systems. These datasets could be orders of volume bigger than conventional datasets that demand more thought at every phase of the processing and data storage. And because working with Big Data may exceed the capacities of one computer, this can become a challenge for pooling, allocating, and coordinating resources from a network of computers. It is becoming more importantfor businesses to break data tasks into manageable pieces.

Variety

Problems with Big Data are usually unique because of the broad range of both the sources that the business should process without compromising quality. Data could be extracted from internal data mechanisms such as server logs and apps, from social media accounts of the business, from sensors embedded into the physical device, as well as from other providers. One of the primary goals of using Big Data for business is to manage potentially beneficial data regardless of the source by capturing then integrating all information into one system.

Big Data is a Big Deal for Business

The rise of Big Data could lead to new business management concepts. During the early days of professional business management, executives discovered that the minimum efficiency scale was an important factor to define competitiveness. Similarly, future competitive advantages are more likely to be developed by businesses that could not only gather better and more data but can also use the captured information at scale.

By contemplating on these issues as well as areas of concerns below, business executives will be able to determine how Big Data can help their businesses move forward including the scope and speed of the change that is now crucial to success.

Areas of Concern in Using Big Data for Business

Transparency

As information becomes more easily available across different industries and sectors, it could pose a threat to businesses that relied on proprietary information as a competitive asset. For instance, the real-estate business relies on information like exclusive access to buyer profiles. Data acquisition, in this case, needs considerable effort and expense.

However, in the present day, web-based real-estate specialists begun to ignore the need for agents, which allows buyers and sellers to exchange viewpoints on the real estate value and building easily-accessible data.

Another area of change is setting up of some companies of easily-accessible satellite images, which when processed and assessed, could contain clues about the physical facilities of their competitors. This visual data could provide insights about expansion plans or even restrictions such as shipping routes, the capacity of the facility, and other valuable business insights.

But the biggest challenge is the fact that the huge volume of information businesses have captured is often hidden in organizational silos such as communications, manufacturing, engineering, or RD, and this impedes immediate evaluation of data to guide the business.

Hoarding of data within the business could also be a critical concern. For example, numerous financial firms lose a lot of money because they do not share data among various lines of business like money management, financial markets, and loans. Usually, this impedes these businesses from building a singular view of the market or gaining deeper insights about a customer. Some manufacturing companies are trying to break these silos by integrating data from several systems, encouraging collaboration among divided units, and even soliciting feedback from their customers, vendors, and other stakeholders for developing new products and services. In large manufacturing businesses like those in car production, different suppliers are providing thousands of parts. By integrating data platforms, car companies can easily collaborate with their supply chain partners as early as during the design stage, which is a key factor to reduce the cost of manufacturing.

Decision Making

Big Data can also change the way we decide for our business. Through regulated experiments, businesses can easily test their assumptions and evaluate their results, so their operational changes and investment decisions are guided. As a result, experimentation could help business executives to determine causation from the simple correlation of data, which could reduce the differences in results while also improving product performance and finances.

Data-driven experimentation could also take several forms. For example, leading online stores are regular experimenters. In certain scenarios, online businesses assign a set of their online views to implement experiments, which disclose the factors that drive higher sales gains or user engagement.

Large businesses who are also selling physical goods also use several data-driven experiments to aid in their decisions, which could be elevated to a new level using Big Data.

For example, McDonald's are known to equip several of their outlets with devices, which capture operational data as they monitor customer behavior, store traffic, and best-selling items. Researchers could model the effect of variations in the menus, store designs, and staff development programs to the overall productivity and revenue.

If you think that it is impossible for your business to conduct controlled experiments, you can still use natural experiments to figure out the sources of variability in performance. For example, you can capture data on several groups of employees who are doing the same level of work at various sites. By simply making the data accessible, employees who are lagging behind can be more encouraged to enhance their performance.

Market Segmentation

Businesses who regularly need to face customers have used data for market segmentation and targeting. By using Big Data, your business can be capable of real-time personalization, which may take a lot of investment in the past. Online retailers are now capable of monitoring the behavior of their customers from their click streams, so they can update their preferences, and model the possible customer behavior in real time. By doing so, online retailers can easily recognize if customers are ready to buy and so use nudging strategies to complete the process. Online businesses can also use this real-time targeting for their rewards program to increase purchases of higher-margin products.

Data-driven business is prevalent in the retail industry because of the emergence of the volume of available data from online purchases, social media engagements, and location-based smartphone conversations.

But other business sectors can also take advantage of new data analytics with the rising complexity of analytical tools for further segmentation of their customers.

Business Management

Big Data can expand the possible domain of application for algorithms as well as machine-mediated assessment. Some manufacturing companies, for instance, managers are using algorithms to evaluate sensor data from assembly lines, which build self-regulating processes, which can reduce waste, prevent expensive and risky human interactions, and of course to increase revenue.

In advanced oil fields, devices regularly interpret data on pipelines, wellhead conditions, and other important machines. The data will be analyzed by groups of computers that feed their results for real-time operation centers, which adjust oil flow for optimizing production and minimizing downtime. By using Big Data, oil companies can save between 10 and 30 percent while lifting the production index by at least 5%.

The products that range from personal computers to oil drills could now capture data that could indicate how the company is using them. Businesses could assess the raw data, and in some instances, instantly resolve software glitches or assign service personnel to fix the issue. There are companies today who specialize in capturing and assessing data to dispatch preemptive repairs so that the problem is handled before it could affect the business operations. The captured data could also be used to conduct product changes, which could avoid future problems or to supply customer-use inputs for developing new products or services.

Through Big Data, the business could experience improved performance, better management of risk, and the capacity to discover insights that could help in advancing the business. As the cost of acquiring and using communication devices, sensors, and software for data analytics continue to fall, more and more businesses will use Big Data for managing their operations.

New Business Models

Big Data has spawned new types of businesses that encompass data-driven business models. Most of these businesses are positioned as intermediaries in the value chain where they can find the creation of valuable exhaust data generated by business processes. For example, a transport firm realized that in their operations, they were capturing large volumes of data on worldwide product shipments. Recognizing the value in the data that they have captured, the business developed a unit that sells the data as supplementary information for business and economic forecasting.

Another worldwide enterprise learned a lot from assessing its own data as part of a manufacturing turnaround that they realized they could do business doing the same work for other companies. Today, the company is aggregating supply-chain data for their manufacturing customers and is now selling software tools to enhance their performance. In fact, the service business is now doing well compared to its manufacturing business.

Chapter 2
Big Data: A Critical Key in Business Growth

Because of our growing interconnectivity, every sector, especially in business is woven with data. Like other crucial elements of business productivity such as human capital and hard assets, many of today's business activities may not be completely functional without data.

The use of Big Data - huge volumes of information that you can bundle together and assess to figure out patterns and guide you in business decisions - is now becoming the deal-breaker for competitive industries. Effective use of big data can help a business grow by improving productivity and building significant value for the global economy by eliminating waste and increasing the quality of products and services.

It used to be that it was only data scientists get excited over the sheer volume of data processed every second around the world. However, the business world is now gradually sharing the same excitement. Based on research conducted by McKinsey & Company Global Institute, the torrents of data produced, preserved, and utilized for business insights has become a critical element to advance not only businesses but also governments as well as the public.

The record of past trends in innovation and investment in data and its influence on productivity and competitiveness strongly reveals that Big Data can be a critical element to trigger the next wave of changes in the world.

The same pre-requisites that paved the way for previous IT-driven innovations enhancing productivity, as well as parallel innovations in business management, are all geared towards Big Data. It's not surprising that providers of Big Data technology and suppliers of advanced data analytics will soon find their place in the global economy.

Businesses should invest more in Big Data as doing so can help them create value and become more competitive. For instance, large retailers who have invested in Big Data years ago, now see the opportunity to increase their operational margins by at least 50 to 60%.

Big Data as a New Competitive Advantage in Business

Using Big Data is now becoming a critical factor for large businesses to get ahead of the game. In many industries, large players and new players alike are now using their leverage for data-driven strategies not only for business innovation but also for competition and providing value.

Many successful large businesses today have invested on Big Data during its early years. For example, in the healthcare industry, pharmaceutical companies who have pioneered the use of Big Data thoroughly analyzed the product's effects on health, and so they were able to discover the benefits as well as risks that were not captured by small clinical trials.

Other Big Data pioneers used data from trackers embedded in their products from industrial goods to kiddie items to figure out and analyze how people actually consume these products. Such results guided these businesses to create new services and design new products.

Big Data can also help in creating new opportunities for growth and even in completely new categories of businesses. In fact, even the aggregation and analysis of business data have brought forth an entirely new industry itself. Most of the service providers in the data analytics industry are positioned in the middle of large data flow where raw information about products and services, consumers, suppliers, could be gathered and analyzed. Business leaders who are forward-thinking must start building their organization's capacities for Big Data.

Aside from the mere volume of Big Data, the high-frequency and real-time nature of data are also crucial. For instance, the concept of *nowcasting*, the capacity to project metrics like consumer intent, within minutes, is now becoming intensively used, which has added considerable power to projection. Meanwhile, the high level of data frequency will allow businesses to immediately test their theories in near real-time and to a level that has been considered impossible just a few years ago.

How Can Businesses Leverage Big Data?

There are five main ways that businesses can use Big Data as leverage: transparency, data accuracy, product and service precision, guided decision-making, and innovation. These areas will be comprehensively discussed in this book with more focus on how you can use data analytics for business advancement.

1. Transparency

Big Data can reveal considerable value by ensuring transparency. There is still a remarkable volume of data that has yet to be transformed into digital form; this includes paper files or data that is intentionally not made easily accessible in networks. Some businesses are still spending at least 25% of their operational expenses on searching for information, and then transmitting this information to a virtual location, which can be quite inefficient.

2. Accuracy

As businesses produce and store more data in digital format, they also capture more accurate and more comprehensive performance information on everything from product catalogs, to billable hours, and thus enhance performance and expose variability. Leading companies are now using their ability to capture and analyze Big Data to perform controlled experiments for better decisions in management.

3. Service and Product Precision

Big Data can help businesses to segment their customers, and so they can better customize their products and services.

4. Guided Decision Making

Comprehensive analytics can significantly improve decision-making, reduce risks, and discover valuable insights that might remain undiscovered without effective data analytics.

5. Innovation

Businesses can use Big Data to develop innovative products and services. For example, manufacturing companies are now using information captured from sensors that are embedded in products to build cutting-edge customer service like proactive maintenance to prevent issues in new products.

How Big Data Is Used to Create Value

Consider this: experts believe that if the United States Healthcare System can use Big Data to advance quality and efficiency of service, the sector is capable of creating about $300 Billion in value annually. About 60% of that will be an 8% reduction in the expenditure on healthcare.

Meanwhile, in European countries, government administrators will be able to produce more than $ 120 Billion by using Big Data to improve their operational efficiency. It is interesting to take note that this does not include using advanced data analytics to decrease the instances of errors and fraud and boosting tax collection.

However, it is not just businesses and organizations that can gain from the value created using Big Data. Consumers and the public can also benefit a lot from Big Data. For example, consumers of services enabled by personal-location data could create $600 billion in consumer surplus.

One of the most widely-used services powered by Big Data is the smart routing based on real-time traffic data. With the rise of smartphones and easy-to-use navigation apps, experts believe growth in the area of smart routing. By the year 2020, around 70% of smartphones are GPS enabled, which represents at least 20% of growth in 2010.

According to estimates, the potential worldwide value of smart routing in the form of fuel and time savings is about $450 to $500 Billion in less than a decade. This represents time savings to drivers of about 20 Billion hours or at least 10 hours each year for every driver and around $120 Billion on fuel savings.

Another considerable potential in generating value from Big Data is from integrating separate data pools. For example, the United States Healthcare System has four main data pools: separate departments manage claims and cost, clinical, patient sentiment and behavior, and medical R&D. Each data pool. Experts believe that if the US government efficiently uses available Big Data management and data analytics, such as assessing records of actual medical procedures, their costs and outcomes can guide doctors on which type of treatment to provide, and that can actually help save time and money.

Meanwhile, the yearly productivity of the sector can increase by a surplus of 0.7%. However, achieving this productivity boost will require the integration of data from various sources - usually from organizations with no background of scalable data sharing. The system should also integrate data sets such as clinical claims and patient records.

Doing this will generate benefits not only for the different players in the healthcare industry but also for the patients who will have wider, clearer access to different healthcare information, which empowers them through information. Patients can compare not only the cost of drugs, medical procedures, and doctor fees but also their relative efficacy, which enables them to select more effective and suitable treatments according to their molecular and genetic makeup. To achieve these broad benefits, healthcare consumers should accept some level of trading their personal information to access the benefits that integrated data pooling can provide.

Concerns about data security and privacy are just among the obstacles that businesses need to resolve to maximize benefits for the government. Among the most critical problems is a considerable shortage of people who have the skills for data analytics. Per labor statistics, the US may face a deficit of around 180,000 people with comprehensive analytical training and around 1.5

million people who can frame and make sense of data for business decisions.

Of course, there are also technological concerns, which should be resolved so the business world could make the most of big data. Different formats and standards usually hinder the integration of data as well as the application of the more comprehensive analytics, which create value. On top of that, using large digital datasets will need the setup of technological layers from storage and computing through visualization and analytical applications.

Most importantly, access to data should be wide. Businesses will require access to data from external providers such as customers or business partners and continuous integration. A critical competency for data-driven businesses in the future is the capacity to develop great value for data sharing.

Chapter 3
Data Analytics in the Business World

There are three main categories when it comes to data analytics: predictive, diagnostic, and descriptive. Every category is distinct in the value it offers and in how it could be used in business to advance productivity and revenue. It is crucial to understand each category and know the right timing for using a category.

Predictive Analytics

In predictive analytics, we need to make sense of why certain things happened and then build a model to project what could happen in the future, hence the name. The predictions could be in the micro-level such as in:

"There's a 60% probability that our biggest supplier in the East coast will partner with our competitor next year."

It could also be on a macro-level approach such as in:

"Revenue in the Eastern coast will likely to increase by 6% to 9% in the next year."

Predictive analysis can be remarkably beneficial for businesses as it can serve as a guide in making their operations more efficient by cutting down on the costs. The process can also make certain that businesses could preserve the resources needed to take advantage of future opportunities.

More micro-level forecasts like customer-level estimates of returns could be used to determine which resources should be prioritized and build support strategies with integrated sales and customer support.

For instance, a B2B business who is working with several clients in a certain industry may largely depend on their individual relationship with each customer.

The business can work with each client to create models, which can forecast which client has the highest intention to build the business again. Equipped with this data, the business could better assign their resources to the most important clients and those with the highest potential for retention.

But studies reveal that most businesses depend predominantly on descriptive analytics, which we will discuss next.

Descriptive Analytics

As the name suggests, descriptive analytics is more about summarizing and reporting data. This type of data analytics is geared towards what is currently happening or what has already happened. A sample data set extracted through descriptive analytics include "top 10 customer service representatives in terms of processed requests for the month of July in Asia." Businesses can use descriptive analytics, especially those that are just initiating analytics of various data produced internally.

For example, one company discovered that they had spent about $10 million per year on different sales training programs. The outcome of the descriptive analytics was a mere summary of the expenditures, but still, it was useful because they learned an important data about their spending on sales training. They may not have yet the data to determine which program provides the highest ROI, but they can implement a plan to analyze which programs must be dropped and which must be duplicated and expanded to maximize revenue.

Diagnostic Analytics

In contrast to descriptive analytics, diagnostic analytics is less focused on what has occurred but rather focused on why something happened. In general, these analytics are looking for the processes and causes, instead of the result. Here is an example diagnostic analytics "Revenue is up in the East coast, and the likely reason is the increase in investment on targeted marketing approach, employment of professional sales agents, and the closure of a major competitor in the area."

Take note that descriptive analytics cannot provide an answer to important questions such as "How can we avoid this problem" or "How can we duplicate this solution?" Diagnostic analytics covers these.

One application of diagnostic analytics is in the field of sports. For instance, in the Major League, many teams have ditched away from assessing the pitchers on the number of runs they allow. Based on gathered data, the rate that the pitchers allow runs (result) is more likely to be less consistent compared to their rate of strikeouts and walks (process). The runs for the current year are less closely related with the runs allowed last year compared to the strikeouts and walks last year.

Successful baseball teams are now focusing on the process instead of the outcome, so they can better assess the talent of the pitchers and determine which team they should trade or acquire. It may cost about $6 million to $8 million to sign up a free-agent pitcher, so understanding whether his skills really caused his performance can be helpful for League teams.

Data-Driven Business is Crucial for Predictive Analytics

The data revolution is growing rapidly. Not only is the volume of data growing, but there are also a lot of changes in the ways businesses use data for advancement. According to the recent report released by the International Data Corporation, global data increases by about 200% every two years. Also, by the year 2020, global data will reach more than 44 Trillion Gigabytes, which was 1000% increase from the data in 2013.

Aside from data explosion, an increasingly digital economy and advances in data science significantly enhanced the analytic value of Big Data. Hence, businesses could better access data for improved predictive power as well as high-impact results.

Corporate use of predictive analytics is increasing because many businesses now understand the value that data and analytics could offer for their decision-making. Based on one estimate, businesses in the top levels in their respective industries are 6% more profitable and 5% productive because of using data analytics. By using predictive analytics, business executives can make significant discoveries about their companies and resolve complicated business problems, which could enable the business for strategic decision making and performance.

Before you can maximize the benefits of predictive analytics, your business should be capable of using the right type of data, analytic sciences and a culture which empowers your people to determine and understand insights, and then use these insights for strategic decisions. The challenge in creating this business setting is bridging the gap between business and data science. Making sense of data is often easier said than done, and many businesses have tried creating data-driven workplace, but they don't know how to get there.

Based on the results of the study conducted by KPMG, about 54% of business executives believe that the primary hurdle to success is determining what type of data to capture, while 85% say that they don't know how to make sense of the data they have captured.

Predictive analytics can provide a competitive edge if the company captures the right data and then its staff knows how to understand and apply data-driven insights to advance growth.

Companies that are seeking to produce meaningful business insights should shift from better and bigger data and balance their analytics with perspective. This change could require setting up a state-of-the-art data experience by capturing the right data, leveraging analysis to maximize data and building a culture that is capable of integrating insights into everyday business processes as well as decision-making.

Choosing the Right Data to Deliver the Right Business Insights

Before starting the analysis process, businesses should identify, assess, and integrate the data, which are most informative and valuable for their growth. This process could pose a remarkable challenge because it could be quite difficult for leaders to determine on which of their numerous sources of data to concentrate on to resolve business concerns and extract the most beneficial strategic business insights. Companies should have a well-established foundation of reliable and rich data to make strategic decisions.

First, businesses should determine the right mix of data, research, and alternative sources that should be captured for their business needs. Business executives also have to create a well-structured curation process, which includes sourcing, assessment, filtering, record-keeping, and maintenance.

For example, one manufacturing company experienced and remarkably solved their dilemma in this area. The main product was placed at the beginning of the supply chain, and the production was laborious. Hence, the business requires an accurate production process for its end-customer demand to adjust its budgeting and operation in the nick of time. But company leaders also had to consider the considerable shifts in the customer demand because of a highly sensitive emerging market and an over-dependence on their sales data, inventory, and internal operations. They had to evaluate consumer data earlier to adjust their operations as needed.

The business resolved this problem by integrating added data sources and predictive factors like macro-level data, online search trends, and other crucial data sets about the economic perspectives of the consumers and their spending patterns. By investing into its sourcing process and capturing the right data, the business enhances its predictive accuracy by a stunning 150 percent.

The Right Analytics Could Solve Critical Business Problems

When businesses have the right data sets, they have to determine the right analytical sciences and processes according to their needs. For instance, retail analytics like pricing optimization research or customer demand could be the ideal focus for a business that needs to assess its pricing strategy. Meanwhile, a business may take advantage of people analytics if it has to assess turnover risk management or recruitment studies. Meanwhile, a growing division in business may have to require operations analytics like new product planning studies immediately.

Business executives have to make certain that the analysis and process of the business are well-aligned by using analytics processes to define their structures and systems instead of integrating analytics into their current processes. A carefully selected and well-integrated analysis could provide decision-making support on important business problems and help the business improve its organizational efficiency.

Adopting the Right Culture for Integrating Data Analytics into the Business

Most businesses - regardless of whether they are just starting their data analytics investment or have already achieved some mastery - are realizing that their culture may not be suitable enough to manage and apply the heavy stream of data. Based on one estimate, around 60% of big data investments may fail to go beyond piloting and experimentation because of issues on company culture.

To convert data into enhanced operational effectiveness, businesses should have a data-driven culture, which could send insightful and well-defined messages to their people. If your people don't have a vision, and they don't understand the essence of working on big data - or if the ideal processes are not yet established to enable employees to make improvements - your initiatives for data analytics are likely to stall.

The right business culture should be initiated by the business leader who must support and emphasize a data-driven culture, which can be done by establishing a clear big data strategy.

Another strategic move for promoting a data-driven culture is to understand the readiness of the business for data analytics or how well the data systems, process, and your people are aligned. This comprehensive perspective on the analytics level of the business as well as the insights on how to boost the growth of a data-oriented company - could enable business executives to maximize and grow the data analytics of the company.

The Importance of Managing the Life Cycle of Full Data Analytics

One company implemented this kind of data experience assessment after they have invested in big data. They have acquired state-of-the-art data analytics technologies, and they have created a new data science division for the company. However, 3 out of 5 business executives said they were not successful in extracting the needed data for business decisions.

Even though the business executives believed that the data they have captured is enough and they have used recent technology, the evaluation revealed the more pressing problems of the business, which includes process management and communication. The company discovered that they don't have the capacity to manage the full lifecycle of the data analytics from requesting to a decision. Hence, their investment in data analytics was not set up for success in the very first place.

To resolve the issue, the business had to adjust its focus. The business leaders launched a new management program that could better align its executives and data division when it comes to accountability process, decision-making systems, capacities, and service level agreements. The outcome was increased adoption of analytics for strategic decisions.

Starting Small in Data Analytics

One company revealed their plan of launching a large-scale data analytics investment. The business leaders were excited about the possible capacities that they can acquire like real-time reporting, data integration across several platforms and assessment of large-scale information. However, the business has not yet figured out the specific problems that they want to be addressed. Furthermore, they did not have any plan for what they want to actually do with the data and the insights they want to achieve.

Considering the time and money associated with launching a large-scale solution, a business should consider whether setting up small programs around certain problems and then scaling up is the ideal approach for the organization. Launching a small-scale data initiative, when you are only exploring the area, can provide some actual benefits once you do it correctly because the business could find its analytical basis and learn what it really requires from technology, management, data, and resources viewpoint.

Furthermore, a small application on a particular problem could allow the business to appreciate the Return on Investment of its analytics strategy better before it could scale up to a larger model.

Below are some important questions that a business must answer in trying to decide about the magnitude of its data analytics investment:

Effective use of data analytics requires a lot of data management skills. These may include conducting complicated analyses, but also managing storage of data as well as integration, transforming business problems into data analytics, and summarizing actionable business insights into a platform that can be understood by all stakeholders. If your business does not have the required skills today, it will never instantly learn them all because you have invested in analytics.

What are you doing with the insights that you have already processed from your captured data?

A business that has ignored data-oriented insights will not suddenly start leaning towards data because the insights begin arriving in real-time. If you are not yet data-oriented, beginning with a smaller project could win support, show business value, and drive taking action on insights before you can invest in a large-scale solution.

What particular problems you encounter could be solved by data analytics?

Try to project the business value for the given problems that the data analytics would likely help in solving and try to see if it can justify the investment. The guaranteed bets are those in which the returns are high and depend only on the known concerns. Try to be exhaustive in listing the business problems that you are trying to solve because it will inform staffing and cost, system requirements, as well as implementation. If your list has several problems - or usually low impact issues - you might get results by knocking off individual issues with small-scale data systems.

Are you aware of how the data analytics process could help you solve the business concerns?

Many business leaders struggle with making sense of data science. However, you should still have a solid grasp on the projected impact of the solution and how it could fit into the analytics strategy of the business. Materializing the value of data analytics could require a lot of moving parts aside from the technology and tools, although it could be enticing to believe that the new solution could solve the puzzle. Your business should be clear about the problem that the data analytics solution will address, similarly to what particularly will be done with the outcome. Meanwhile, if you think that the solution may feel like a large feat, then you might consider testing the waters first.

Who will use the insights?

Even professional data scientists and analysts could be overwhelmed if you ask them to gain mastery of new data analytics solutions while working on their current projects. Take note that the magnitude of the solution is proportional to the disruption that you could see. If your business is not yet ready to hire a specialist staff, you may not be able to maximize the benefits of the new solution. In such case, the business may be better off adding small-scale programs, especially if the returns are more apparent.

Finally, you should understand that any data analytics solution that you want to implement may never enhance your returns. Your bottom line will improve if professional analysts find business-oriented insights and if dynamic, data-oriented culture will act on these insights to grab business opportunities. Without these pieces in their proper places, implementing a solution and expecting an analytics strategy to rise is much like buying eggs and hoping that a bike will just appear. You still have a lot of work to do before you can see the results that you are looking for.

Chapter 4
Tools, Technologies, and Trends in Business Data Analytics

At this point, you might have already been convinced that big data is not just a fad, but a new business factor, which you must incorporate into your strategic planning and operational plan. You should already have strategies in place to manage huge volumes of structured and non-structured data. And with the emergence of big data also comes the need to make sense of it in a way that it will bring actual business value. Business executives who already began the process by resolving management issues are now ahead in finding ways to use big data to identify patterns, detect trends, and assess other valuable discoveries from the ocean of data that they can use.

With the excitement over data analytics, you may be tempted to just purchase software for big data analytics, assuming it could be the answer for the business needs of the company. However, the technologies used for big data are not enough to cover the expected outcome.

Your business must first have a well-established analytical process, and your staff should have the required talents and skills to maximize the technologies needed to implement the initiative for data analytics. Acquiring added tools beyond the current intelligence and application of the business may not even be suitable if you revisit your business goals.

Moreover, technologies and tools are still emerging, and some of these technologies have yet to be calibrated for business use. However, you should also not ignore the fact that big data and analytics are changing at a fast-paced that you might experience the dilemma of betting on the viability of the data analytics or face the risk of being left behind.

Several years ago, new business technologies might have taken decades to be dominantly absorbed by businesses. But today, business owners are using solutions in a matter of months and even weeks.

In this Chapter, we will discuss the top emerging technologies, tools, and trends that you should consider for your business.

Cloud Computing

Hadoop is a framework and toolsets used for processing huge volumes of data sets. It was created for working on physical machinery. But this has changed through time. Today, a rising number of tools are available for businesses who need to process data in the cloud. Most businesses will soon process data through an integration of cloud and on-premises.

For example, a marketing agency that specializes in SaaS-based commercial analytics moved from an in-premise Hadoop and database structure to a cloud-based data warehouse. The company captures online and physical retail sales as well as client demographic information and real-time customer behavior. The company then assesses the data sets to help businesses create customized messages that could drive the expected response on the part of the customers. In most instances in real time, this is done all in near real-time.

Cloud-based data storage was cost-effective for the company as the business requires comprehensive reporting features for structured data. And as a hosted solution, this is scalable and quite easy for the business to use. It also helps the business's bottom line as it is relatively cheaper to expand on the virtual database than purchasing physical machines.

Meanwhile, Intuit was careful in using cloud data as the business requires stable, secure, and an environment that is susceptible for easy auditing.

As of the moment, the company is storing and processing its data inside their private cloud. But still, moving into the cloud is still inevitable for Intuit as it is offering products that are running in the cloud. The company has to face the need to shift all the data to a private cloud.

Data Lakes

The conventional concept for database states that you should build first the data set before you fill in any form of data. This model is turned on its head by the concept of Data Lake where you can take all the sources of data and save them all into one repository without designing first a data model. Rather, it offers tools for businesses to assess the data, along with a generalized description of what type of data is existing in the lake. This data model is organic and incremental for creating a large volume of databases as businesses are building the views into the data as they move through the process. However, the people who should use it should have the right skill sets.

Some Silicon Valley companies today are using Data Lakes, which includes clickstream user information and business and external data. However, the usual concentration is on how to democratize the tools to enable the business to maximize the data set. But among the many concerns in this type of technology is that it is not yet business ready. Users are still looking for capacities that conventional business databases are offering such as encryption, keeping track of access control, monitoring the lineage of data from the origin to the destination.

Hadoop

Distributed frameworks for analytics are now shifting into a distributed form of resource managers, which are slowly shifting Hadoop into a data operating system that could be used by the business in general. Using Hadoop, the business can initiate various data manipulations and operational analytics by using the system for file storage distribution.

What is the advantage of this for your business? As most data analytics tools, such as SQL and in-memory can run on Hadoop with sufficient performance, more businesses will use Hadoop as a data hub. The capacity to operate different types of queries as well as data operations against the information stored in Hadoop will be more cost-effective.

Faster SQL on Hadoop

If you know how to code and you are comfortable in working with mathematical expressions, it will be easy for you to fill in data and analyze anything stored on Hadoop. But if you are not, then you need someone who can place the data into a language and format that you can understand as a business executive. This is where SQL for Hadoop could come in handy.

Data analytics software that can support SQL query can allow you to understand the data. Basically, SQL on Hadoop can open the door to

Hadoop for business use. Hence, you may ditch away from the need to invest in getting the services of highly-skilled data scientists and data analysts who could write scripts using Python, Java or JavaScript, which is something that users of Hadoop have conventionally had to perform.

Predictive Software

With data analytics, businesses can work with data and acquire the capacity to manage large-scale information with different attributes. In conventional learning, data tools are using statistical analysis according to a portion of a total data set. Today, businesses can take advantage of very large numbers of data sets with various attributes for every record, which could increase predictability.

The integration of big data, as well as predictive analysis, will allow businesses to explore new behavioral data several times a day like location or website visits. Data scientists call this sparse data because, in order to look for something that is interesting, you still have to swim through an ocean of information that may not be relevant.

It can be impossible if you try to use conventional machine-learning statistics against this level of data. This is now not only possible but cost-effective for businesses. Formulation of problems can be quite different when you are not thinking about speed and memory. Businesses can start figuring out which variables are best for analytics by driving large computing resources to resolve the business problem.

Businesses can benefit a lot from the ability of the Hadoop for real-time analysis. The main concern has been the speed of response, with Hadoop taking about 20 to 30 times longer to respond to queries compared to more established technologies. Hence, businesses are attracted to new software technologies such as Apache Spark and Spark SQL. The latter comes with graphics and streaming features and can respond to queries faster compared to Hadoop. It preserves the data inside Hadoop, but it still provides enough performance to close the data gap.

Deep Learning

Deep Learning is a set of machine-learning strategies that are established on neural networking. This technology is still evolving, but it shows great promise for businesses. It enables computers to identify items of interest in large-scale of binary and unstructured data and to analyze relationships without the need to enter program instructions.

For example, a deep learning algorithm that analyzed Wikipedia information assesses on its own that Texas and California are both American states. The technology was able to do this without the programming concepts of a country and state, which is a big difference between the rising deep learning strategies and traditional machine learning.

Big Data can now perform things with many diverse and unstructured data through advanced analytical strategies such as deep learning to help businesses. For instance, it can be used to identify different types of data such as the colors, shapes, or particular objects in a video. In fact, in 2012, Google was able to accomplish this by using an algorithm that can identify pictures with cats. This concept of advanced analytics, cognitive engagement, and its applications to business are crucial technologies that could help an enterprise to gain a competitive edge in the future.

NoSQL

NoSQL is a set of databases that is rapidly rising in popularity as software for use in certain types of analytical applications. This technology is the alternative to the conventional SQL databases. About 20 to 25 NoSQL databases are available today, and many of them are open-source. One example is ArangoDB, which is a NoSQL product with graph database capacity. This product provides a faster and more direct way to assess the network of relationships between sales personnel and customers compared to the ordinary relative database.

SQL databases that are open source have been available for a while, but they are just only rising in popularity because of the analytical needs of businesses. For example, one company has added sensors on their store shelves to keep track of the available products, the period of how customers are handling them and how long customers are standing in front of certain shelves. These sensors can drive data streams, which can exponentially grow.

In-Memory Data Analytics

Businesses are now using in-memory databases to hasten the processing of data analytics. Many enterprises are already using hybrid analytical and transactional processing, which allows data to be stored in the same in-memory database. However, there is some sort of hype around in-memory data analytics, and some businesses are overusing this technology. For analytics where you need to access similar data, in the same way, several times a day - and you can't see any remarkable movement in the data - in-data could be regarded as a luxury.

And although it is possible to work on analytics a lot faster with in-memory data, all processes should be kept inside the same database. The issue is that many analytics investments today are more on placing transactions from different processes together. Just placing this all on a single database will have you revert back to the old concept that if you want to use in-memory data, you need all your transactions in one place. It is still important to integrate various data sets.

Furthermore, working on one database for the in-memory system could mean that you have to manage, secure, and determine how you can integrate all data sets and set-up for scalability.

How to Stay One Step Ahead of The Game with Business Data Analytics

With many rising trends for using data analytics for business, you have first to set-up the right conditions, which will let your people experiment on your datasets. You must have an efficient system to assess, prototype, and integrate some of these data analytics technologies into the business. Your company's IT personnel should not use lack of maturity as an excuse to do away with experimentation.

On the onset of adopting data analytics for your business, you can empower your top analysts to experiment. Then, these top talents must all together figure out the right time to deliver new resources for the advantage of the business.

Moreover, your IT division should not always depend on analysts who want to try every emerging technology. Your IT personnel should work with your analysts to balance between experimenting new technologies and adapting to business analytics trends.

Chapter 5
The Importance of Data Mining in Advancing Business

Data mining is an analytical process that you can use for your business to convert raw data into relevant information that you can use. By using specialized tools, you can detect patterns in large-scale information to learn more about your customers and in response, develop more effective strategies. The ultimate goal is to increase your revenue and decrease expenditures. Effective data mining relies on efficient data gathering and storage as well as analytical processing.

Retail shops such as grocery stores and supermarkets are the most common users of data mining. Many retailers are offering loyalty rewards, which allow their customers to buy items at reduced prices or accumulate points. The loyalty cards could make it easier for these businesses to monitor who is purchasing what, the time that they are shopping it and at what price margin. The business could use this information, after doing some analysis, for several purposes such as providing customer coupons specifically targeted to their purchasing intent and deciding when to place items on sale or when to sell specific products at a higher markup.

Data Warehousing

Data Warehousing refers to the process of centralizing the data into one program or database. Using a data warehouse, a business could spin off segments of the information for certain users for analysis and implementation. But in other cases, analysts may begin with the kind of data they want and set-up a data storage facility according to these specifications. Effective and efficient management of data will allow businesses to make guided decisions.

Special Analytics Software for Data Mining

Software that is specially designed for data mining can analyze patterns and relationships in data according to the specifications requested by the business. For instance, data mining software could be used to develop classes of information. For example, let's say a grocery store likes to use data mining to identify the right time to offer certain products. It refers to the data it has captured and creates classes according to customer visits and what they have purchased. In some instances, data mining specialists may look for clusters of data according to logical relationships, or they study associations and patterns to make conclusions about consumer trends.

Data Mining Strategies for Creating Value for Business

There are several kinds of analysis that a business could do to retrieve valuable data. Every type of business data analytics will have varying result or impact. The type of data mining strategy you must use really depends on the kind of business problem that you want to address.

Different forms of data analytics could result in different outcomes and so offer different insights for the business. Among the most common ways to retrieve valuable insights is through the data mining process.

In developing your data analytics strategy, it is crucial that you are clear on the definition of data mining and how it could help your business. Take note that the most essential goal of any process of data mining is to search for relevant information, which could be easily understood in large-scale data sets.

Below are the most common types of data mining analytics that you can use for your business.

Anomaly Detection

Anomaly Detection refers to searching for information in a set of data, which cannot match an expected behavior or predicted pattern. Anomalies are also known as exceptions, contaminants, outliers, or surprises, and they usually offer actionable and crucial information. Outliers are objects, which could considerably deviate from the general average inside a dataset or integration of data. In numerical terms, this is separate from the rest of the data, and so the outliers could signify that something is not right and needs more analysis.

Detecting an anomaly in a data set can be used to figure out if there are risks or fraud inside critical systems and they all have the attributes of interest to a data analyst, who could also advance the analysis to determine what is really happening.

This can help the business to find crucial situations indicating fraud, flawed process or areas where a specific strategy may not be effective.

It is crucial to take note that in large-scale data sets, a small portion of anomalies is quite common. Anomalies may show bad data, but it can also be caused by a random variation or may even show something that is statistically interesting. In these situations, more analysis may be needed.

Clustering Analysis

Clustering Analysis refers to the process of detecting data sets with similar attributes to learn their similarities as well as differences in the data. Clusters have specific traits in common, which could be used to enhance algorithms for targeting. For instance, clusters of customer information with similar purchasing behavior could be targeted with similar services and products to try raising the conversion rate.

One outcome of clustering analysis is the development of customer personas, which refer to fictional characters identified by a business to represent the various customer types within a specific demographic. This includes the behavior set or attitude of customers who are actually using the brands or products. The business can use a specific software or programming language to work on relevant cluster analysis.

Association Analysis

Association Analysis will allow the business to discover relevant associations between different variables in a large-scale database. This data mining strategy will allow you to discover concealed patterns in the data, which could be used to detect variables inside the data as well as the co-occurrences of various variables, which exist in different frequencies.

This data analytics strategy is commonly used by retail stores to look for patterns within information from POS. These patterns could be used in recommending new products to others according to what other customers have purchased before or according to the types of products that are purchased together. When you do this correctly, you can help your business increase your conversion rate.

One good example is Walmart's use of data mining in 2004, in which the retail giant discovered that the sales of Strawberry Pops increase at least seven times before a hurricane. As a response, Walmart placed this product at the checkout counters when a hurricane is about to strike in an area.

Regression Analysis
In Regression Analysis, you can try to determine the dependency between attributes. There is an

assumption of a single-way causal effect from one attribute to the response of another attribute.

Independent attributes could be affected by each other, but this doesn't mean that there is a mutual form of dependency. By using a regression analysis, the business can identify if one variable is dependent on another but not the other way around.

A business can also use regression analysis to identify the various levels of client satisfaction and how this attribute can impact customer loyalty and how the service levels could be affected, for example, the current weather.

Another good example is how dating sites use regression analysis to better offer services for their members. Many dating sites are using regression to match two members according to a list of attributes to find the best partners for them.

Data mining could help businesses to look for and focus on the most relevant and important information, which could be used to establish models that could help in making projections on how systems or people could behave so the business could make some projections.

By gathering more data, you can better build models that you can use to effectively implement data mining strategies, which will result in more business value for your business.

Classification Analysis
Classification Analysis refers to a systematic approach for gathering crucial and relevant information about data. This type of data mining analytics can help the business to determine which set of data can be used for further analysis. Classification analysis is often used alongside cluster analysis as classifying data is usually the pre-requisite for clustering.

Email providers are among the common users of classification analysis. They are using algorithms, which can classify email as useful or spam. This could be done according to the data that is connected with the email or the data that is inside the email, for instance, specific works or attached files that signify spam.

Chapter 6
Data Integration and Its Role in Advancing Business

Data Integration refers to the process of combining data from independent sources, which are warehoused using different tools and usually offers a single perspective of data. Integrating data is crucial in case of merging two businesses or consolidating systems inside one company to get a single perspective of the data assets of the company.

Probably the most common step in data integration is setting up the data warehouse of the business. The advantage of a data warehouse will enable a business to conduct analyses according to the data inside the warehouse. This may not be doable on data available on different source systems, because they may not have the required data, although the data sets may be named similarly.

Moreover, if you want to keep data integration solutions completely aligned with your business goals, then you have to be always mindful of the particular kinds of business value, which could result from effective use of tools and strategies for integrating data.

In this Chapter, we will discuss the top ways that data integration can bring value to your business. I have included several actual cases to show the various types of value that data integration can provide. Hopefully, this can help you explain to your partners or your boss the value of data integration. It could also serve you as a guide on how you can plan and design suitable data integration strategies to advance your business.

Business Practices Values

Let us begin with a more generalized perspective of data integration. Most valuable data-driven practices in business often rely on one or several forms of data integration. There are business processes that cannot be functional without data integration. This is particularly true for data warehousing and business intelligence.

Remember, effective decisions may rely on calculated, aggregated, and time-bounded datasets within a data warehouse, which can never take place without effective data integration. Success in sales, for example, usually relies on a total view of every customer information that is usually aggregated using tools and techniques for data integration.

Moreover, integrating various businesses as well as their processes using shared data should be backed up by a data integration solution. This is helpful whether the businesses are divisions inside one enterprise or different enterprises that can share data from one business to another. Meanwhile, business processes like just-in-time inventory or operational business intelligence should be backed up by efficient data integration solution, which could be used in real time or with few delays. As you try to advance your business, you pace will also accelerate. Data integration could speed up the process to gather and integrate time-sensitive data at speeds that are not even possible a decade ago.

Data Integration and related business processes such as data management and data quality assurance can add value to business data. As a result, the value of business processes will also increase.

Visibility of Data Integration

Identifying the business value of data integration once you see it can be more difficult than you might expect because this data analytics process is usually separated a level or two from the systems that your business might be using. But in general, the data integration value is usually visible as valuable data. Below are common examples of data integration in this value field:

- A business executive who access a single view of customer information, which was built with data integration through data sync.
- A business intelligence user entering a query into a data warehouse and the system responded with complete data models and metadata that were set up using data integration
- Several business supervisors are accessing information on a computer that is updated real-time or as needed through a data integration solution.
- A product supervisor accesses a list of available supplies from a supplier within a data set, which the supplier established through data integration and delivered across business boundaries through business to business exchange.

Even if data is accessible in a Graphical User Interface (GUI) or a report, business users may forget that data integration may overlook that data integration provided the information. Many business executives fail to realize that data integration is responsible for collecting, preparing, and delivering most of the data that you may take for granted. Nowadays, Data Integration is a fast-changing discipline, which offers data for several types of applications whether they are operational or analytical.

Collaborative Business Practices of Data Integration

To ensure that Data Integration offers the best type of business value, the system must be aligned with the goals of the business that is relative to the data. Fortunately, several collaborative practices have emerged in recent years, so data specialists could easily streamline their work with broad range of colleagues.

Data Governance
Data Governance refers to data integration processes that focus on privacy, security, risk, and compliance. However, many businesses have

expanded Data Governance to also cover quality, standards, architecture, and many other issues on data. The team working on Data Governance could help data scientists to get a single view of business goals that are relevant to data and align their work properly. Meanwhile, the change management process of Data Integration can enable Data Integration specialists to think of possible solutions to increase data value.

Data Stewardship

Data Stewardship is designed for managing quality of data by identifying and prioritizing quality of work according to the needs of the business and certain parameters such as technological capacity and budget. The person who is in charge of the data, also known as the data steward, should work together with business and technical people. Through the years, data integration specialists have used stewardship into their array of strategies for better credibility in alignment and prioritization of data integration work.

Collaborative Data Integration
Collaborative Data Integration is a loose strategy for coordinating the tasks of data integration teams, which include data specialists. In general, collaborative data integration uses applications and practices like code review, team hierarchy, project management, and software versioning.

Unified Data Management
Unified Data Management is a recent business practice, which aims to coordinate tasks across several data management disciplines described above. UDM also enables collaboration between business management and data management to ensure that most data management tasks add business value by supporting business management goals.

What Data Integration Can Do for Your Business

The outcome of data integration is quite ubiquitous in the business world, which enables commercial activities. However, we often don't identify these activities to consider data integration as a crucial process in today's business.

If your business needs to confirm the value of data integration (a common requirement for sponsorship, investment, or approval for data integration), then you have to educate your partners or your boss the critical role that data integration could play for your data-driven business processes.

Data Warehousing and Business Intelligence

As a support system of data warehousing, data integration can add value to the business process. Through data integration, you can collect raw data from different sources and combine them all to develop new products. A data warehouse will contain data and data sets that do not exist anywhere in the business.

Moreover, because of the requirements of business intelligence, data that goes into the warehouse should be regularly reconfigured to develop calculated, aggregated, and time-bounded data, established into multi-channel datasets. Data Integration cannot collect data itself; rather it can shift the data into these necessary structures.

Data integration for business intelligence will allow high-value processes. A data warehouse constructed through data integration allows decision making at tactical, strategic, and operational layers. Data created through data integration is crucial to Business Intelligence strategies such as dashboard reporting, performance management, advanced analytics, and online analytics. These data warehousing and business intelligence activities - also enabled by data integration - could help in customer retention, increasing sales, improving the efficiency of business operations, guide sales, and marketing activities, enable strategic planning, and other valuable business outcomes.

Data Integration Could Add Value to Business Data

Many business owners think data integration as a process of moving data. But those who are trained in data science understand that it is not easy to just move data around. There is a need to improve it. Every ideal data integration solution can add value to the process.

Data integration improves data during the process. Data quality strategies are being added into data integration solutions. This is organic because data integration could filter out concerns about data quality that should be fixed as well as areas for improvement. Data integration can also help in improving metadata, data models, master data, and other attributes of data. Hence, the data could come out as complete, clean, and consistent.

Data integration can also help in building new databases that are valuable for the business. Remember, the data contained in the data warehouse can never be found anywhere else in the business. Similar to the value-adding system in manufacturing, data integration can capture raw material and build them into new data sets. Therefore, data integration can convert data to make it more valuable for more business processes. Aside from moving data, data integration can also convert data, so it is suitable for any target system. To put it simply, data integration repurposes data so more business units, as well as their processes, could be beneficial for the business.

Single, Unified View of Business Entities

Through data integration, the business can capture data from several sources to complete a single view of the entities of the business such as assets, locations, staff, finances, products, and clients. This is on the same level of data warehousing, but this is more on operations and not on business intelligence.

By effectively using data integration, the business can complete its customer profile and improves value to any client-oriented business process from sales and marketing to client support. Complete product data can also add value to business systems for procurement, product management, and supply chain manufacturing.

Data Replication

Data replication, also known as data synchronization, is another data integration system that can help add value to the business. For instance, data replication may build a complete view of a central data hub for access by several users and applications. This is seen in central hubs for product data, customer data, and master data. Replication may also enhance relevant data across several applications and their databases. For instance, client-facing applications for contact centers can be limited to a partial view of a customer, unless a total view can be developed by replicating customer data across these applications.

Data's business value in replication is that more business owners have a more unified view of a separate entity like finances, customers, and products. Yet, data replication systems may tend to move and integrate data more often, usually several times in a day. This hastens the freshness or data currency in applications. Hence, data is not just complete but also updated, which is crucial for businesses that need current data for their decision making.

B2B Data Exchange

B2B Data Exchange is a promising area for development because businesses can use data integration tools and strategies in areas where these could be rare. Many data exchanges are low-tech and manually entered, which should be replaced in order to be synchronized. Experts project a wide modernization in data exchange between businesses, especially in product-centric enterprises like retail, suppliers, and manufacturing. This is also crucial for financial institutions, healthcare, and other organizations who are using procurement and supply chain systems.

The need to modernize data exchange between businesses is an urgent concern. However, there is also the need to develop business value in this area. In general, business partnerships are crucial to advance businesses in terms of market reach, revenue, and brand development. Business partnerships can grow by achieving better operational excellence through data integration.

Real-time Delivery of Data

Businesses need to adapt to the fast pace of the world, and data integration can help in integrating data at speeds that are even impossible a decade ago. Real-time data delivery that is usually enabled by modern data integration systems can enable several high-value business processes.

Businesses are now using applications to monitor data such as business activities, facility status, grid monitoring, and so on. These can be quite impossible without the real-time capacity of information delivery supported by data integration.

Operational business intelligence often captures data several times a day from operational applications and makes the data available for monitoring and other kinds of management or operational reports. This provides the business to access data for strategic and operational decision-making.

Chapter 7
Data Visualization

Particular attributes of data could only be understood if they are presented in graphic form. Data visualization or the art of representing data in visual form is crucial to transforming raw data into a sensible data that can be used by the business.

To achieve real learning from data, business executives should know how to use visualization techniques to explore data and communicate the meaning of data to the rest of the business. In this Chapter, we will examine the process of visualization, as well as the people and technological skills needed for the business to make sense of data.

As we have already discussed in the previous chapters, businesses today are capable of capturing data at a fast rate mainly for reporting, compliance, and visualization. However, genuine value could only be achieved if the information has been processed, understood, and finally acted upon by the organization. Without an effective system for data processing and presentation, data is just data with no value for the business.

For many businesses, the development of data visualization technology followed a familiar journey: basic charts and tables done manually were replaced by Excel or Numbers, which was then succeeded by conventional business intelligence systems such as databases that can present information easily and as needed. These presentation features started as reports and were soon replaced by interactive platforms.

But with the rise of big data conventional business intelligence technologies may fall short if analysis, discovery, and visualization capacities are more subtle. The market for data visualization has increased remarkably in the past few years as a way to provide insights into complex and large-scale datasets.

Basic data exploration tools are among the emerging areas of business intelligence, and the more conventional business intelligence software developers are innovating their products for the business user. Moreover, with the rise of powerful computers, smartphones, and tablets, people can interact with their data easily than in the past.

To put it simply, visualization capacities will enable the business to interact easily and understand big data. Data visualization is very effective in business because people are naturally attracted to visual analysis. We are highly-suited for identifying visual patterns, and our brains are hard-wired for what we see to process better understanding.

Through data visualization, the business can also integrate large-scale of information in a single place, which allows people to make sense of numbers and text better.

Areas of Data Visualization

To become a more effective tool, a business should invest in three important areas of data visualization: process, people, and technology.

Process

The system of developing data visualization such as a poster or an infographic involves a lot of discipline and may even require different sub-systems that should be well coordinated. An essential step is to establish the ultimate goal of the data visualization right from the start.

People

Business owners should remember that people are closely related to the process. Hence, a wide range of skills is important to create an effective visualization. The skills needed for this are mainly drawn from data mining, statistics, computer science, graphics and also psychology.

Technology

With the range of technological options available in the market, selecting the right data visualization tool could be overwhelming, especially for business owners with no background in the area. This is the reason why you should first establish your goal to narrow down the wide categories of technologies available including business intelligence tools, graphics tools, analytics tools, and other tools.

In its raw form, data is just data, and it can only become valuable once you analyze it, make sense of it, and act on it according to its suggestions.

Hence, as the scale of data being captured increases, so does the need for visualization to be understood and communicated effectively.

Businesses should invest in the capacities to learn from the data through visualization. But before you can do this, you should understand the whole importance of the process, people as well as the technological requirements. These three areas are integrated with one another, so the business should work effectively to combine these areas to work on one goal.

Experts believe that in the future, data visualization will become more interactive, real-time and accessible by everyone in the business. As new technologies emerge and data visualization becomes more advanced, business executives should be able to respond faster and better.

And as data becomes more interactive, it will be easier for anyone to explore the numbers easily without exerting too much effort or background in data science. The business can improve interactive and real-time data visualization so it can leverage the platform to reach more people such as customers, partners, stockholders, and so on.

Furthermore, improvements in technology could make visualization a lot easier to develop, which could allow more people to access visualization. Your business should continually develop its systems to adopt visualization as a mode of communication and data exploration.

This will not only enhance data visualization improvement in the long-term. This will also offer businesses with the information and understanding they should learn from their data and act accordingly.

Advantages of Using Data Visualization for Business

One important attribute of a competitive business is the ability to make decisions as fast as possible. But before a business can achieve that, business leaders should have access to data in real-time and interpret it accordingly.

Gathering information and the capacity to understand it is crucial for businesses. To detect business opportunities earlier than competitors, the business must be able to access, assess, understand, and respond to information faster and more effectively than ever before.

The tools and strategies for data visualization can enable the business and its team to work on new strategies to significantly enhance their skills to grasp data hiding in the layers of information. Below are the top five advantages that data visualization can provide to business owners.

Visualize patterns and connections between operations and sales and marketing activities

Among the important advantages of data, visualization is how it can enable business users to more easily detect relationships as they happen between sales and marketing performance and business operations. In the highly competitive nature of the business world, looking for these relationships within the data has never been crucial.

For instance, let's say a business executive for a toy company is reading the monthly customer information. The executive can access a bar chart, which shows that the net promoter score of the business has decreased by three points in the past quarter in Japan. The report suggests that there is a concern with customer satisfaction in the country. However, the report lacks on insight to explain why the ratings got dipped.

By offering a more comprehensive report of the business as well as operational dynamics, data visualization allows the leaders to see that the recent events in Japan have affected the customer satisfaction. The capacity to make such connections will allow the business leader to determine the real cause of the concern and respond faster for resolution.

Make Sense of Data in New and More Innovative Ways

According to research conducted by the University of Pennsylvania School of Medicine, our eyes can transfer information at about 10 mbps, which is about the same speed as internet connection. However, many business reports are presented for business executives who may fail to understand the data because these are filled with plain charts and static tables that cannot supplement the information.

On the other hand, data visualization allows end users to absorb a large-scale information about business and operations. Effective visualization will allow business executives to identify relationships between multi-faceted data sets and offers better ways to make sense of data by using fever charts, heat maps, and other helpful and relevant graphical representations.

Businesses that are using visual data are more capable of finding the information they need once they need it and can do so more effectively compared to their competitors who are not using data visualization.

According to a market survey conducted by Aberdeen Group in 2013, business managers who are using visual data tools have 28% more chance to find relevant information compared to their peers who are relying on dashboards and traditional reports. Furthermore, about 48% of business intelligence users are businesses who are using visual data can find the information they need even without asking the help of their IT personnel.

Detect and Respond on Rising Trends Faster

The scale of information that businesses are capable of capturing about their customers as well as market trends can offer business executives with relevant insights into new opportunities to do business and increase revenue as long as they can spot on opportunities in the layers of data. By using effective data visualization, business executives can detect sudden changes in customer behaviors as well as market conditions across several data sets much faster.

For instance, marketing executives for a grocery chain could use data visualization to see that customers are willing to spend more as the economy improves and they are also more interested in buying organic items that are more expensive compared to regular items.

A more comprehensive analysis of customer behavior and other data sets suggest a rising opportunity for the store to launch a special section of organic products. Business insights like this can enable the organization to respond to this new business opportunity ahead of its competitors.

Tell a Story

Another benefit of using data visualization for business is its capacity to tell a story that everyone in the business and its stakeholders can relate to.

For example, business executives for a manufacturing company who are monitoring crucial indicators like net profit margin and EBITDA. They could only view a part of the story pertaining to the current conditions of the business through a bar chart, which may not show that the business already produced 2% revenue growth for the previous month. This report doesn't show which specific categories are increasing or decreasing as well as the probable reasons why.

A heat map can show which product categories are performing or underperforming, and will enable business executives to consider the data to figure out the factors that are shaping sales. The data could reveal that cosmetics are not performing, but that higher-income segment comprises the majority of sales. The business can use this insight to target marketing efforts to this customer segment to increase conversion rates as well as profit growth in this category.

Communicating business executives with data visualization could open better ways of looking at operational and business data, which enables senior management to find new opportunities while enabling a wider audience of analytics with the goal of advancing the business.

Directly Interact and Control Data

Among the top advantages of data, visualization is how it could provide actionable business insights. Unlike static charts and tables, which you can only view, data visualization will allow users to control and interact data.

For instance, a traditional business report can inform a business owner of an appliance company that sales for coffee makers for July are down. But the report cannot inform the owner why sales of coffee makers are down or if specific brands or price are doing better compared to others. Furthermore, the data contained in the report might represent the situation days or weeks ago, so the data is not accurate and does not signify the current trend.

Through real-time predictive analytics integrated with data visualization, the business owner can view current sales figures and check why specific brands are not performing well as well as the possible reasons that revenues are lagging behind - for instance, sales campaigns launched by competitors.

The business owner can identify the best action according to the analytical models that can be developed specifically for the business. For instance, he may launch a month-long sales promo for certain dealers that are targeted at the most possible buyers with a price that can undercut the competition but can generate acceptable profit.

Chapter 8
Develop Your Own Data Analytics Strategy and Action Plan

The focus of this book is all about big data and analytics and how they can change the way we do business today and in the future. As we use data-driven techniques, they will gradually become a crucial point of competitiveness among different industries.

To fully take advantage of data analytics, businesses should invest more on mutually supportive capacities:

1. Businesses should be capable of identifying, combining, and managing several sources of data
2. Businesses should be capable of building advanced analytics structures for projecting and maximizing results.

3. Businesses should be capable of transforming the enterprise so that the data and models can really lead to better decisions.

Two crucial features underpin these business capabilities: a clear strategy on how we can use data and analytics to beat the competition and execute the right strategy using the best tools and technologies available.

A clear vision of the desired effect on the business is also crucial to shaping the integrated strategy for building framework, data sourcing, and business transformation. This can help you prevent the usual traps of starting the plan by asking what the information can do for the business. As a leader, you should invest enough time and effort to align your staff across the organization to work towards achieving one mission.

Choosing the Right Data to Use

The area of data and data analytics has drastically changed over the years. The scale of data is growing at a faster rate, and we can also see a great acceleration on the opportunities for businesses to expand insights by integrating data. With access to better and bigger data, businesses can have a better understanding of their market. The capacity to make sense of data can improve business operations, client satisfaction, and overall business strategy. This will further help the business in two major areas:

Creative Sourcing of Data

Usually, businesses already have the data they require to resolve business problems, but most business managers are not capable enough to use the information they have in making important decisions. For example, operations supervisors may not fully understand the potential value of real-time supply chain data that they have. Businesses can encourage more comprehensive analysis of data by being particular about the problems as well as business opportunities that they are facing.

Managers should also tackle this area creatively. For example, social media can provide the businesses with terabytes of unstructured and non-conventional data in the form of posts, photos, conversations, engagements, and videos. You should also consider the data streams that flow from sensors, external sources and tracked processes ranging from remote demographics to client satisfaction. One way to encourage better thinking about the possible data is to continuously think about the decisions that the business can make if you have all the data you need.

Empower and Support Your IT Department

Conventional IT frameworks may not be capable enough to allow creative ways of sourcing data, storage, and analytics. Current IT structures may also hinder the integration of separated data and the control of unstructured data usually remains beyond the capacities of conventional IT. It may take years to resolve these issues completely, but businesses can resolve short-term data analytics concerns by working with their IT staff to determine priorities. Hence, you should immediately identify and relate the most crucial data for use in analytics and then launch a cleanup task to integrate and sync information that is overlapping and to fill in missing data.

Building Frameworks that Can Predict and Maximize Business Outcomes

Business data is a crucial but competitive advantage, and performance improvements can arise from analytics models, which allow managers to project and maximize outcomes. Also, the most effective strategy to build a model often begins, not with information but in identifying a business opportunity and figure out how the model could improve performance. Data connections that are widely understood by business managers can generate faster results. Businesses should strive to find the simplest framework that can improve its data processing and analytics performance.

Transforming Business Capacities

The primary concern that business owners often face is that their middle managers are not capable of understanding and appreciating data analytics. Hence, even if a business invests in improving its data capacities, many managers are not using them.

These business problems usually arise because of a mismatch between the current culture and capacities of the organization and the rising strategies to exploit data analytics effectively. The new strategies either are not aligned with how businesses really arrive at certain decisions or fail to provide a clear-cut blueprint for achieving business goals.

Technologies are designed for experts in modeling instead of being easy to understand for people who actually need to use them. Few middle managers also find the models not engaging enough to appreciate them. This is a common mistake of businesses who want the new strategies to permeate the business. Hence, you should take note that using big data requires strategic organizational change, and these three actionable areas can help you achieve your end goal.

Build Business-Related Analytics That Managers Can Use

Most early execution of big data and analytics end up in failure because they are not synchronized with the day to day process and decision making practices of the business. Developers of business models should understand the kind of business judgments that supervisors make to align their actions with general business goals. Consultation with the people who will actually use the data analytics will ensure that the tools are

Conclusion

Knowledge is power, and time is money. It might be just a matter of months before your competitors finally gain a remarkable edge to dominate the market because they have already implemented strategies backed by the effective use of data analytics. You need to up your game today, and this book was developed so you can do exactly that.

sourcing data, building frameworks, and convert the business culture. This simple action plan can help in sustaining the flexibility of your business. This is crucial because the data itself with the technologies and tools for management and analysis will continue to change, which will provide your business with more opportunities. As more businesses are learning the core skills of using data analytics, establishing state-of-the-art capacities will become your competitive edge in advancing your business.

Integrate Data Analytics in Basic Tools Used by Front Line Managers

Business managers require transparent approaches for using the new frameworks and analytics every day. As needed, layers of data and complex modeling are needed to improve marketing, operations, and risk control. The important element here is to divide the software developers from the managers who will use the data-driven platforms. Remember that your goal here is to provide your frontline staff with the right tools and platforms that can help them to do their jobs a lot easier instead of the other way around.

Businesses should now act now to integrate big data and analytics not only in their operations but to most of their organization - sales and marketing, customer service, finance, employee engagement, and so on.

However, instead of implementing a massive change, you should focus first on specific tasks in complementary with current decision processes, so businesses could effectively manage investments and risks.

Build Businesses Capacities to Take Advantage of Big Data

Even with basic and usable models, many businesses should improve their analytical skills and capacities. For analytics to become part of the daily operations of the business, your managers should view it as a crucial source of resolving issues and identify business opportunities. Execution may vary according to the goals of the company as well as the desired time frame. Synchronizing mindsets and cultures usually need an interdisciplinary approach, which includes role modeling by business leaders, training, metrics, and incentives to reinforce the behavior you want.

Other Books by Author

You can check out Jeff Reed's other books at his Amazon Author Central profile
Click here or go to: http://bit.ly/JeffReedBooks

[Blockchain: The Essential Guide to Understanding the Blockchain Revolution](http://bit.ly/JeffReedBooks)

[FinTech: Financial Technology and Modern Finance in the 21st Century](http://bit.ly/JeffReedBooks)

[Investing in Ethereum: The Essential Guide to Profiting from Cryptocurrencies](http://bit.ly/JeffReedBooks)

[Smart Contracts: The Essential Guide to Using Blockchain Smart Contracts for Cryptocurrency Exchange](http://bit.ly/JeffReedBooks)

www.ingramcontent.com/pod-product-compliance
Lightning Source LLC
Chambersburg PA
CBHW061441180526
45170CB00004B/1503